In this WMG Writer's Guide, *USA Today* bestselling author Dean Wesley Smith takes you step-by-step through the process of writing without an outline and explains why not having an outline boosts your creative voice and keeps you more interested in your writing.

The
WMG Writer's Guide
Series

The Write Attitude

Writing into the Dark:
How to Write a Novel without an Outline

Discoverability: Help Readers Find You
in Today's World of Publishing

Killing the Top Ten Sacred Cows of Indie Publishing

How to Write a Novel in Ten Days

Killing the Top Ten Sacred Cows of Publishing

The Pursuit of Perfection:
And How It Harms Writers

Deal Breakers 2013:
Contract Terms Writers Should Avoid

Surviving the Transition: How Writers Can Thrive
in the New World of Publishing

Think Like a Publisher: A Step-By-Step Guide
to Publishing Your Own Books

WRITING
INTO THE DARK

HOW TO WRITE A NOVEL
WITHOUT AN OUTLINE

A WMG WRITER'S GUIDE

DEAN WESLEY SMITH

WMGPUBLISHING

Writing into the Dark

Published 2015 by WMG Publishing
www.wmgpublishing.com
Cover art © copyright Peschkova/Dreamstime
Book and cover design copyright © 2015 WMG Publishing
Cover design by Allyson Longueira/WMG Publishing
ISBN-13: 978-1-56146-633-7
ISBN-10: 1-56146-633-6

First published in slightly different form on Dean Wesley Smith's blog
at www.deanwesleysmith.com in 2015

For all the brave writers out there writing stories into the dark.
Have fun.

Contents

WRITING
INTO THE DARK

HOW TO WRITE A NOVEL
WITHOUT AN OUTLINE

A WMG WRITER'S GUIDE

INTRODUCTION

In almost 150 novels now in both indie and traditional, I have written into the dark on some, done outlines on others, and even did a 135-page "fully realized" outline on one poor novel.

There are as many ways to outline a novel as there are writers. Plus, there are about a million books out there giving you the secret to outlining. In some of the online workshops I help with at WMG Publishing, I even taught a few ways to outline.

But there are very few articles and books on how to just type in the first word and head off into the dark writing a novel with no plan, no character sketch, nothing but pure exploration.

That's what writing into the dark is all about. Pure exploration of a story.

In this book, I hope to help you learn how to have the courage and the ability to just tell a story from your creative side.

SO WHAT EXACTLY IS WRITING INTO THE DARK?

Some call it "writing by the seat of your pants." There are other terms for it that are so stupid, I can't bring myself to even type the names of them.

Basically, writing into the dark means that you decide to write a story without an outline.

Now most short story writers do this automatically. But faced with a novel, the same writer who just had a blast going off into the dark on a short story will freeze down like shallow lake in the Midwest in the dead of winter.

Critical voice takes over the writer's mind, and all the stuff the writer was taught by people who have never written a novel comes roaring in.

In fact, most of us in our early years of writing take all our information and learning from very, very unqualified people.

English teachers in high school may know how to put a sentence together in some grammatically correct fashion, but they have zero, or less than zero, idea how to create a story from nothing.

We are taught how to tear stories apart under the guise of learning, but that's like handing some kid a hammer and telling him to tear down a house. Then when the house is in rubble, you turn to the kid and say, "Now, build a wonderful new home with fine craftsmanship there."

The kid might have been fine at tearing a house apart, but tearing a house down teaches little of the creative process, the building process.

So teachers tear apart a book, then make students outline the book. What that does is make the writer of the book look damn smart, actually. Students come away from the process thinking,

"Wow, how did the writer know to put all that foreshadowing in chapter six for what's going to happen in chapter ten?"

So then, later, when the writer is facing a novel, the writer thinks all that idiocy taught in school is going to help the writer with the task of writing. Nope.

In fact, most of that learning from school will hurt the creative writer.

But off the writer goes, spending time and energy outlining and working on the outline and making sure the outline is perfect before ever writing word one. And all that is done from the critical voice, from the voice of a teacher who wouldn't have been able to write a novel on the threat of death.

It is any wonder so many early outlined novels fail, and fail big time?

And actually, most outlined novels never get written. I'll talk about why later in the book.

CRITICAL VOICE VERSUS CREATIVE VOICE

A great deal has been said about critical voice versus creative voice in writing, or in any art, for that matter. Great art is rarely, if ever, created from a critical perspective. Art is never done purposely.

Great art comes from the creative side of our brains. I like to think of the creative part living in the back of our brains. The front part of our brains, the critical part, is what takes in all the information. The creative part has a large filter and only takes in the knowledge it wants and uses.

The creative side of our minds has been trained since we were born, and story has been trained into that creative side since we were first read to by our parents. The creative side loves story.

For most writers, the difficulty comes when trying to get past the critical side of our brains and write from the creative side only. Outlining comes from the critical side by the very nature of outlining.

So the critical side of our minds outlines a book, then we wonder why the creative side often doesn't want to follow the outline. The creative side knows story, knows what needs to be in a story.

So all the way through this book, I'm going to be talking about how to access the creative side, how to trust that part of your mind to create stories, and how to kill the fear that the critical voice will use to try to stop you.

Much, much more on this topic coming up.

WHY WRITE INTO THE DARK?

The first answer to that question is easy. Writing into the dark imitates the reading process for the writer.

All writers are readers. And as readers, we love it when a writer takes us along for the ride in a good novel.

So when writing into the dark, that same feeling of reading is in the writing process. Our conscious mind is just along for the ride. The creative side is making up a story and entertaining us as we type.

Later on in this book, I'll also talk about the many problems that stop outline writers. One major factor is boredom.

Imagine if every novel you picked up had a detailed outline of the entire plot, including the ending, right at the start. Would you read the novel after reading the outline?

Chances are, no. What would be the point? You already know the journey the writer is going to take you on.

4

So as a writer, why do an outline and then have to spend all that time creating a book you already know?

"Boring" doesn't begin to describe it.

And as I said, I wrote a lot of media tie-in books from outlines. My rule during those days was to write the outline, get it approved by Paramount or some other license holder, then never look at the outline and just write the book.

My memory is so bad that after seven to ten months from the time I wrote the outline to the time I got the contract and wrote the book, I had no memory of the book I had outlined at all. None.

And if the title hadn't been on the contract, I wouldn't have remembered that either.

So I never looked at the outline. Never. I just typed in the title and wrote off into the dark. That kept the book fresh and alive for me.

And no editor or license holder ever noticed the book was different from the outline they approved. Not once.

The key is to make a novel fresh to the reader. If the writer is bored or feeling like the book is "work" to write, you can bet that feeling is coming through the words to the reader.

Here is one more reason for writing into the dark: If you have no idea where the book is going, the reader sure won't either.

NO RIGHT WAY

Please remember, as I work through this book, that there is no right way of writing any particular book.

Or only one way for a writer to always work.

There are as many ways to write a book as there are writers.

Writing into the dark is just another option.

In the Thriller Online Workshop that I offer through WMG Publishing, numbers of writers mention to me each time that class is offered that they are surprised that I suggest character sketches and outlines.

And that I suggest taking another thriller writer's novel apart and outlining it to study.

There are some books, some projects, that would be better served with outlining.

No book is the same, no process is the same.

And I have to admit right here, in the introduction, that I outline in my own way, every book I write.

When I have a chapter finished, I jot down who the viewpoint characters are, what they are wearing, what happened in the chapter.

So as I go along, I outline each book as I write it.

I never outline ahead of the writing, but after the writing is done. That keeps the creative side of my brain in control of the writing.

And the real reason I do that is to keep track of what I have already done. And what a character is wearing. And so on.

It also helps my creative mind see the patterns in the book as I write.

So I write into the dark with most novels these days.

But I outline as I go, after I have written a chapter.

That's just my way. Use it if you want.

Now onward into how to get over the fear and critical voice problems that come with typing in a title and just writing a novel into the dark.

CHAPTER ONE

SOME BACKGROUND

The reason there are very few articles or books about writing into the dark is because the process gets such horrid bad press. Just the idea of writing without planning ahead on a project as long as a novel makes most English professors shudder and shake their head and turn away in disgust.

And beginning writers mostly just can't imagine doing that. It just seems impossible.

Yet, many long-term professional writers write this way. And many of the books those same English professors study were written completely into the dark.

So why do all of us, as we are growing up, buy into the idea that novels must be outlined to the last little detail to work?

First, the problem comes from the fact that we all started out as readers.

To readers, writers know it all. They know enough to make that plot twist work, that foreshadowing inserted at just the right place, the gun planted when it needs to be planted to be fired later, and so on.

To readers, writers are really smart to be able to do all that.

Then we get into school and all the English teachers build on that belief system by taking apart books and talking about the deep meaning and what the writer was doing. And that makes writers seem even smarter and the process of writing a novel even more daunting.

So the desire to outline is logical, totally logical, after all that.

In fact, it seems like outlining is the only way to do a complex novel.

But interestingly enough, that very process of outlining often kills the very complex structure the writer is hoping to achieve.

A HUMBLING EXPERIENCE

Two of the most humbling experiences in my life occurred the two times I went into a graduate-level English class at a university as a professional writer. (Do not do this if you can avoid it.)

The first time, the English professor, doing his job, had the students read and discuss two of my short stories BEFORE I GOT THERE.

So two of my stories were deconstructed by fifteen graduate English department students.

So I arrived, talked some about what it was like to be a freelance fiction writer, and then the professor turned the discussion to my two stories they had read. And I started to get questions about how did I know to put in the second hidden meaning of the story, or the foreshadowing of an upcoming event, or…or…or…

They all knew far, far more about those two stories than I did.

Honestly, I could barely remember the stories, and I had no idea I had even put in all that extra stuff they were all so impressed by.

And the reason I couldn't remember is that my subconscious, my creative brain, put all that in. My critical, conscious brain had nothing at all to do with it.

I had just let my creative brain tell a story.

Nothing more.

The problem was that for weeks after that first time into that class, I couldn't get all that crap back out of my head. I found myself wondering about second meanings, about subplots, about foreshadowing—all those other English-class terms. Froze me down completely until I got past it.

Let me be clear here. My critical brain is not smart enough to put all that stuff in. Luckily for me, my creative brain seems to be smart enough if I get my critical brain out of the way and let it.

But getting that stupid critical brain out of the way is the key problem.

BREAKING OUT OF THE TAUGHT PROBLEM

All of us go into writing novels with all that training of thinking we need to know all that stuff about subplots, foreshadowing, sub-meanings, and so on. Thinking about it, I find it amazing that with the training we get, any novel gets written at all.

Or that any writer even gets started writing.

And outlining seems to be the logical process when faced with all that. In fact, outlining would be the only way to let the critical brain even pretend to be smart.

When I started writing solidly, novels seemed flat impossible. I could manage a short story in an afternoon, but anything beyond that was a concrete wall of paralyzing fear.

So how did I break out of the problem of everything I had been taught?

I used to own a bookstore. One fine slow afternoon, I was sitting in the front room of my bookstore and I looked around at all the books in the room. And I had a realization that in hindsight sounds damn silly.

I realized that people, regular people, wrote all those books.

And what all those regular people did was just sit down and tell a story.

They were entertainers.

That simple.

It was no magic process that only really special English-department-anointed people could do. And if all those regular people with all those books covering the walls of my bookstore could do it, then I could do it as well.

So I looked at how I felt writing short stories.

At that point I just wrote a story and stopped when the story was over. Nothing more fancy. I figured I could do that with a novel as well.

So after that realization, over the next few years I started five or six novels and got stuck at the one-third point where I could no longer fight the critical voice into submission. I had no tools to fight the critical voice at that point in time, to be honest.

So two years after that realization, mad at myself for not finishing a novel and for making novels into something "important" instead of just fun, entertaining stories, I sat down at my trusty typewriter and thought only about writing ten pages a day.

I had no outline, nothing. My focus was on finishing ten pages. Period.

Thirty days later I had finished an 80,000-word novel.

My first written novel.

The next day, I started into a second novel, doing ten pages a day again.

I powered my way through the need, the belief, the fear of doing a novel the way it "should" be done.

And never ever had that fear again. I had other fears, sure, but not that one.

Every long-term novel writer has some story of getting past the need for major outlines, for major planning. A lot of younger professionals are still banging out outlines and following them.

Again, no right way.

But eventually, if you are going to be around for a long time and writing, you need to feed the reader part of your brain and just write for fun.

Otherwise, knowing the ending of a novel, having it all figured out ahead of time, is just too dull and boring and way too much work.

CHAPTER TWO

THE CRITICAL VOICE PROBLEM

L et me give you a secret about writing.
Ready?

The only purpose of the critical voice in creative writing is to stop you.

That's the secret, and when you finally take that secret in, you will be on the way to really getting to your real writing ability.

Critical voice in humans is there to protect us.

In writing, it wants to stop you from making a fool of yourself, or from putting out a bad product. (Thus the intense desire to keep rewriting over and over.)

When your critical voice completely succeeds, you are no longer writing and sending out anything for others to read. After all, if someone else reads what you have written, it might be dangerous.

Made-up danger, of course, but to the writer letting the critical voice win, writing feels like very real danger.

In real life outside of writing, your critical voice is a protective mechanism.

In the late 1960s, I found myself standing on the top of a rock cliff near Sun Valley, Idaho, with two other skiers. We were looking at jumping off the cliff and there was a cameraman off to one side to take pictures.

My critical voice was screaming that we needed to check under the snow at the bottom for big rocks.

One of the other guys was suggesting the same thing.

Fear and critical voice had stopped us cold.

The third guy just shouted to the photographer to see if he was ready, then the guy backed up ten steps and skated at the cliff and went off into the air, ski tips down, arms spread, flying like a bird, laughing all the way.

The picture of him in the air off that cliff was in *Ski Magazine*. And he didn't hurt himself.

I skied around. So did the other guy.

The one guy in the picture went on to make a living in Hot Dogging, soon called Freestyle Skiing. He was fearless.

I let my critical voice combine with pure fear to stop me cold.

The best way many people see this concept clearly is in the bad horror movies when a woman in high heels goes into an old mansion where there is a killer. The woman in the high heels needs a better-developed critical voice.

No doubt about that.

(Or the writers need a new plot.)

But unlike going into an old mansion, or jumping off a cliff on skis, there is no danger in writing.

The fearless writers contain their critical voices and write what they love, what moves them.

As I said in the lecture on Writing into the Dark, my critical voice with writing is a tiny little thing whimpering off in a corner of my mind. When it tries to stand up, I throw bricks at it until it goes back to its corner and leaves me the hell alone.

WORK VERSUS PLAY

Writing from the critical voice is work. Plain and simple.

It's why so many beginning writers describe writing a book in metaphors that make them sound like they have just won a major world war all by themselves.

If I hadn't defeated my critical voice, I would have long ago moved on to doing something far more fun than writing from critical voice.

Writing without critical voice turned on, just writing to tell myself a story, is like reading. The process is wonderful and I enjoy the journey.

So what happens when a writer says out loud, "I'm going to write this next novel into the dark. No outline."

That is like giving your critical voice an energy drink or two. That critical voice will find a thousand ways to come at you.

I bet some of you while reading this have already had the critical voice yammering at you about how dangerous this would be.

Remember, the goal of the critical voice is to stop you.

Just remember my friend having his picture in *Ski Magazine* and me carefully and fearfully skiing around that cliff and you get the idea.

Throughout this book, I'm going to detail numbers of ways critical voice and fear will work to stop you, and how to get around them. But at this point I want to deal with one of the major ways that critical voice will come at you almost instantly when you even think of writing into the dark.

WASTED MY TIME

This is a huge killer, and I constantly hear this from new writers. Not only about writing into the dark, but about so many other aspects of writing.

Truth: When you are writing new words, you are never wasting your time.

Never.

Here comes a dirty word. Better cover your ears.

Practice.

There, I said it.

Imagine walking up to some poor kid who is practicing a musical instrument and telling that kid he is wasting his time by practicing. He needs to only play concerts or nothing at all.

Can't imagine that?

Yet when your critical voice tells you that you might be wasting your time, that's exactly what you are saying to yourself.

You are saying your writing must always be special, that it can't be done to practice.

Yeah, believing every word you write is always special will freeze you down into making writing work and then fairly quickly stop you completely.

And again, that's what the critical voice wants.

Critical voice does not want you writing or taking any chances.

Period.

And writing into the dark? Wow, what a chance that would be. Far too much of a chance to take because your writing is "special." Your writing must always be perfect and maybe you had better add in just one more rewrite to be sure.

And maybe one more rewrite after that, because rewriting isn't wasting time.

That italics part, folks, was a sarcastic attempt to show you just how stupid those thoughts are. If you believe all of that was advice, you are beyond my help.

Truth: The biggest waste of time in writing is rewriting. Period.

But that's the topic of another book down the road.

Again, we're dealing with the sneaky critical voice always looking for ways to stop you. And rewriting is a great way.

AFRAID TO TRY

If you are afraid to try a new genre, afraid to try a new method of writing, afraid to try to get your work out to markets or show it to your friends, critical voice is in control and winning.

Period.

Heinlein's Business Rules from 1947 are really interesting when looked at from a defeating-critical-voice viewpoint.

Rule #1: You must write.

To do that, just that simple thing, you must overcome critical voice in many aspects.

Rule #2: You must finish what you write.

Critical voice will keep you from finishing with a thousand tricks. If a story or novel isn't done, it can't be shown and thus can't cause you any (imaginary) harm.

Rule #3: You must refrain from rewriting unless to editorial demand.

Critical voice uses the myth of rewriting to make sure nothing will ever be "good enough" and ready to show anyone.

Rule #4: You must put your work on the market.

Critical voice can think of a thousand ways to make you afraid of the repercussions of mailing or indie publishing your work.

Rule #5: You must keep your work on the market until it sells.

Critical voice does wonders when you get rejections from an editor, and can stop you from putting the work back out. And if publishing indie, some imaginary expected sales figure not hit, or some bad review, will cause beginning writers to pull down work.

Heinlein's Rules of Business were to help writers get past critical voice. The rules really are that simple.

And because of critical voice, those five simple rules are almost impossible to follow.

Of course, your critical voice will instantly start coming up with ways how those rules don't apply to you.

Of course they don't.

Your critical voice knows best.

It knows how to stop you cold, keep you from writing.

That's its job, after all.

CHAPTER THREE

THE JOY OF UNCERTAINTY

I am trying in these first few chapters to establish some basics that I hope will help you drive forward while writing into the dark.

The biggest factor once you get past the critical voice is uncertainty.

Uncertainty, when not controlled and used to push forward, causes problems.

Lots of problems.

When a writer lets uncertainty be a bad thing, it's like tossing open a window and inviting into your writing office all the fears and critical voice you can find. And once in, those fears and critical voice will slow you down and stop you.

Remember, that's their job.

Uncertainty, if looked at correctly and embraced, is a positive aspect of writing into the dark.

So let me battle in this chapter to help you keep that window closed to critical voice and fear. What I want to do is help you understand that uncertainty is a welcome feeling when writing into the dark.

THE BOREDOM FACTOR

From a reader's perspective, when I get to a spot in a book I know exactly how the book will end, I put the book down.

If Kris asks me what went wrong in the book, I say: "The book was on rails."

She'll nod because she understands.

The writer had placed the plot of the book firmly on a set of rails and the ending was as clear as knowing that the next stop on a train ride was the city ahead. No uncertainty in the plot at all, and as a reader, I could see the ending of the book ahead.

So I got bored and put the book down.

Most readers are like me. Not all, but most.

When a reader realizes that they know how the book will end, they stop. It might not be a conscious thought. It might be just putting the book down to go get a cup of tea and never returning to the book.

The dreaded critique from a reader: "I knew what was going to happen."

How do you guarantee that statement will never, ever be made about one of your books?

Simple. Write into the dark.

Duh.

If you do not have one idea of where the book is going that you are writing, there is no chance in hell your reader will ever know.

Books on rails are books that were outlined. The writer knew exactly where the book was going, what the end was, so the writer's subconscious put in all the clues to tell the reader where the book was going, and everything in the book, every detail points to the ending like signs with arrows.

Books on rails are seldom original, either. Books outlined by the critical voice just can't be. The critical voice isn't your creative voice. Your critical voice can only dig up old ideas and old plots and parrot them back to readers already familiar with the plot.

So you are writing into the dark to stay original and you don't know where the plot is going.

How does that make you feel as a writer?

Uncertain, of course.

But if you want your book to be original and fresh and have no reader really know where it is going, you need to embrace that uncertainty feeling.

WHERE DO I GO NEXT?

I can hear the doubts, the questions.

If you don't know where the book is going, how do you know what to write next?

In the next numbers of chapters, that's going to be a major topic. I'm going to give you a bunch of ways of figuring that out.

But right here, early in the book, let me tell you the simple answer.

Write the next sentence.

And then write the next sentence.

I am not kidding.

It really is that simple.

What rule anywhere tells you that you need to know what is happening fifty pages away? No rule.

English teacher training or some such nonsense, more than likely.

Just write the next sentence that follows logically through the character from the previous sentence.

And repeat until you find the end of the story.

With every step of that path, with every sentence, uncertainty will be dogging you.

That's a good thing.

But at the same time, don't let the uncertainty be a fear-excuse to stop you writing.

Just write one more sentence. You can do it.

Then write one more sentence.

Repeat.

You know the drill.

It really does work.

UNCERTAINTY AS A SPORTING EVENT

For those of you who know me, know some of my past, you know I have been, and sometimes still am, an adrenaline junkie.

Professional hotdog skiing, professional golf, professional poker, jumping out of airplanes, rafting rivers, starting businesses, three wives, and so on and so on. Never a dull moment in my life, and I lived it that way purposely.

I sort of wonder at people with bucket lists. If there's been something I wanted to do, I just went and did it. I got nothing to put in some stupid bucket.

So here I sit getting adrenaline out of writing. I have fired into my own monthly magazine, I am building a new writing career at the age of sixty-four, and a new business as well.

So is it any wonder that the uncertainty of writing into the dark makes writing fun for me?

Adrenaline is everywhere, with everything I do, including all the learning I get from talking with writers on my blog.

I find the fear of not being able to come up with something to write great fun.

And you know, it's not often that sitting alone in a room and making stuff up can give you an adrenaline rush. (Queue all the porn jokes right here…)

I JUST DON'T KNOW WHAT IS NEXT

What happens when you can't even think of the next word to write, let alone the next sentence?

Your subconscious just won't let a word be written and you won't let your critical voice into the picture.

What do you do?

Again, in later chapters, I'm going to talk a lot more about all this sort of thing, how to get going again, and so on, but here, early in the book, I want to give you a basic writer trick you can use when that happens.

Sleep on it.

But before you call it a night, start off by taking a short break. Sometimes just five minutes will get you back to the next sentence.

And do not focus on how you need to end the chapter, or some plot thing. Just focus on trying to figure out what the character would do next.

What is the next sentence?

If you get back to the computer, do some methods I will outline later in the book, and the next sentence still doesn't come, then go take a nap.

Or go to bed.

The key to this is that as you stand up from the computer, tell yourself you'll have it figured out in the morning, or when you wake up.

Sometimes a five- or ten-minute nap will be enough for me to fire onward after being stuck.

However, the real problem with getting stuck like this is the uncertainty. Getting stuck, which will happen numbers of times in any novel or story, allows in all the doubts, the questioning of the very idea of writing into the dark.

It is getting stuck that causes so many writers to say, "I can't write into the dark. I always get stuck and then I have to outline."

Letting in your critical voice at that point is the worst thing a writer can do.

A writer must learn to trust the creative voice.

Sometimes that creative voice needs a little time, a short nap, a night's sleep, to get untangled, but it will get untangled if you keep the fear and critical voice away.

It is at that stuck point that you need to really embrace and enjoy the uncertainty.

Getting stuck is part of writing into the dark. It is part of the process, a natural part of the process of a creative voice building a story.

Embrace the uncertainty of being stuck, trust your creative voice, give it a few moments' rest, and then come back and write the next sentence.

What almost always happens for me after these rest points is that the book will power forward faster than I can type.

My creative voice has got it figured out and is off and running.

When a book does that, it's great fun.

Enjoy the adrenaline rush.

Remember that being stuck is normal.

And that this writing into the dark process is uncertain.

But one great side of writing into the dark: Your readers will never know the ending of one of your books.

CHAPTER FOUR

WHAT DO YOU NEED TO GET STARTED?

For this chapter, I'm going to go over a list of what you need to get started writing into the dark on a novel.

Some of these points are pretty basic, and some are more difficult.

But a simple list and explanation seemed to be the best way to get you at least mentally ready. All of these points will come up at different points throughout this book.

Be warned: Your critical voice will not like any of these. And if you find yourself disagreeing completely, you might not be ready yet to write off into the dark successfully.

You might be. But I wouldn't bet on it.

FIRST...YOU NEED A LOVE OF STORY

If you are still in that silly early stage of beginning writing where you think you need to read everything critically, you might not be ready yet to tackle a book into the dark.

By reading critically, you are feeding that critical voice with every sentence you read. And, of course, most stuff you read isn't good enough. That's the nature of the critical voice.

A writer like Cussler or Patterson or Nora Roberts or Grisham can entertain millions of readers with every book, and you and your overhyped critical voice will think they can't write at all. That's critical voice turned on far too high and your ego far, far out of control.

You must get back to reading for enjoyment, for the sheer love of a good story told well.

You won't like all books, but your dislike will be for taste, not critical voice. And that's fine.

So if you haven't read a book lately and gotten so lost in the story that you haven't seen a word of the book, then writing into the dark might not be such a good idea until you can get back to really loving to read for the sheer pleasure.

When you can read a book and not see a word of type, then you are ready.

And if you automatically copyedit everything you read, go get help. And I mean real help, professional help, because you have lost all ability to see a story and are trapped by the little black marks on the paper. You can't even begin to be a writer from that mindset, let alone a creative writer, let alone write into the dark.

But if you enjoy story, love to read, and can't see the words when reading because you are lost in the story the writer is telling, you will be fine moving forward and into the dark with your writing.

SECOND...EARLY PRECONCEPTIONS CLEARED

All those preconceptions of the need to consciously put in foreshadowing or plot arcs or character threads or rising and falling tension. You know, all that English class crap you were taught by people good at deconstruction but shitty at creative work.

You must have most of that cleared out, or at least under control in your mind. It is why I talked about it early on in this book.

Studying books, studying plot threads, studying rising and falling tension is one thing for writers to do *after* they read a book and like it.

But you can't come at a book, ready to write a book, with the idea you are going to put that all in.

You have to know that the desire to consciously put in all the literary crap is your critical voice, the thing that is out to stop you cold.

For writing into the dark, the critical voice needs to be ushered into a closet and the door slammed until the book is done.

Your creative voice will put all the stuff that needs to be there in the book, and make you look really, really smart to English classes later. And as I discovered, you won't even know you put that stuff in there for those deconstructionists to find.

But to actually give your creative voice permission to put that all in, you need to take all that sort of stuff out of your critical mind. Focus on only having fun telling a story.

Be prepared to just let the creative voice have its day.

Really hard to do.

Impossible to do if you are reading critically.

THIRD…YOU NEED TO UNDERSTAND YOU WILL WRITE EXTRA

When writing into the dark, the story will often come in parts, and sometimes the parts aren't in a real order. That's part of the fun. And later on in this book I'll explain how to deal with all that.

Sometimes, like a reader, you experience the writing process from word one to the last word. But sometimes, like a cave explorer, you have to see what is up a certain cave until it dead-ends into a rock wall. Since you are walking into the dark, a dim flashlight your best guide to see the step ahead, you won't know until you find the dead end that you were on the wrong track.

That's normal.

And sometimes what you find on that little side trip is valuable to the story and your subconscious took you up that path for a reason. Again, never let the critical voice in to second-guess the subconscious. Just be prepared to accept writing some extra.

For me, in many books, I write very little extra. But for some reason, in my Thunder Mountain series, I tend to write a lot extra.

I have two reasons for that. One is that I am used to writing those bloated, longer books under contract that New York wanted me to write. And to get a story up to length, I would often have to just add in plot sidetracks.

I hated that, and with my own books, I won't do that. A story is as long as a story needs to be.

Period.

But with Thunder Mountain, complex time travel Westerns, I love the setting and the time period, so I have often put my characters on their horses and thought "Wow, wouldn't it be fun to go off the trail and see what's over there?"

(I like doing that in real life as well, but since I have stuck Kris in wilderness areas one too many times, I can now only do that when I am alone in the car.)

What happens in my novels then is that when I am done, my sidetracks are just things I put in for myself. No plot reason, and my subconscious says, "You had your fun, get that out of my story now."

So in that series, I often write a bunch of side roads just for myself.

And I accept that and enjoy it.

Expect to write extra, for whatever reason, when writing into the dark.

FOURTH...YOU ARE *NOT* GOING TO REWRITE THE BOOK

That's right.

Do not give yourself permission to fix anything later.

Do not give yourself permission to write sloppy.

You are writing a book. Period. When you are done writing, you release the manuscript to your first reader and proofreader and move on to the next story you want to tell.

I will explain later in this book some ways to help you produce clean copy as you go along. But you cannot allow your critical voice in any fashion to get anywhere near the book you are writing into the dark.

You can't allow that critical voice to glare in the window, saliva dripping from the teeth, just waiting to get hold of the poor manuscript. That's a quick way to make writing into the dark worthless.

And that includes permission from the critical voice to write sloppy or a second draft.

Otherwise there is no reason to write into the dark. You just might as well outline the poor, sad book and let the critical voice kill it that way.

Yeah, I know, I can hear the screaming now.

And why are you screaming???

Really ask yourself that question. Why are you objecting?

Critical voice, right?

All those English teachers taught you that rewriting is the only way to create real art. Those teachers who couldn't write a creative sentence if forced at gunpoint. Those same ones.

And you bought into that myth.

So answer one simple question: Why you do not believe that you, the creative writer, can write a book from the creative side of your brain without that critical voice pissing all over it?

As I said a moment ago, later in this book I will show you some methods on how to produce clean copy as you go so that when you get to the end, you release and start thinking about the next story.

But for most, this will be the hardest part of writing into the dark.

There is no point at all writing into the dark if you are going to give your critical voice permission to ruin what you did.

And that permission will kill all the enthusiasm of the creative side as well.

And the entire process will fail.

All because you bought into a myth and believe your creative brain just isn't good enough.

Sad, really sad.

CHAPTER FIVE

HOW TO GET STARTED

One of the established facts of novel writing is that almost no writer can hold the plot of an entire novel in their mind. We just can't.

So even if you are outlining ahead, you are spending most of your time just focusing in on one area of the book, one scene, one chapter.

I have a reminder on my wall above my computer:

Write Scenes

That sign was meant to keep me from trying to think about an entire book, or too far ahead in a book.

The sign under the first sign is:

Trust The Process

Can't believe how many times I repeat that to myself when feeling uncertain.

Trust the process. Just trust the damn process.

It's like a signal to my subconscious to come out and play.

That's all fine and good, but how to get started with the actual writing? That seems to be the scary question we all face with every book or story.

SOME ACCEPTED WAYS

In writing book after writing book on this topic, the same basic answers come up about getting started.

They all say that you need one or more of the following:

—An idea

—A cool setting

—Cool character

—Great first line

Okay, those sometimes help. For me, a cool title helps as well.

But if I had to wait around for a cool idea or a cool first line like Billy Crystal in that movie *Throw Momma From the Train*, I would be dead.

So sure, all those things help. But then what?

How do you really get started?

For the answer to that, let me back up to the basics of every opening in any story or chapter.

You must have a character in a setting.

Readers read for characters and all characters must be in something besides a white room.

So to get started, stick a character in a setting. Cool character or not. Cool setting or not.

Just a character in a setting.

Period.

Sounds simple, doesn't it?

Nope. Far, far from it.

THE DEPTH WORKSHOP

The most important and successful workshop I do through WMG Publishing Online Workshops is the Depth Online Workshop.

Here is how to think of depth when writing openings.

Imagine a lake. All beginning writers just try to get their readers to go out across the top of the lake. But the surface of that lake is the line that allows a reader to leave your story. If the reader gets above that surface line, they put the book down.

A simple image.

A story with depth is one that the writer takes the reader and drags the reader under the surface and down the steep slope to the bottom of the lake. And then the writer has the reader follow the story along the bottom of the lake.

From the bottom of that lake, it is a long way to the surface and the writer can do all sorts of things without fear the reader will surface and leave the story.

So the worst thing you can do it just let your readers water-ski across the top of the water. You want your readers deep in your story, with no chance they will leave.

That is called depth.

And it takes me six weeks and five assignments and a ton of examples to show writers how to do that in that Depth Online Workshop.

So back to the question on how to start a story.

Take a reader quickly down into depth.

Those who have taken the online workshop know how that's done.

For everyone else, let me just say this:

Depth is caused by having a character be firmly in a setting with opinions and all five senses and emotions about the setting.

None of this can be from a writer's perspective.

It all must be inside a character's head.

AN EXAMPLE

A few months back I wanted to write another Thunder Mountain series time travel novel. I always start those novels with new characters, but I had no character, no idea of a character, nothing. I just had a title: *Lake Roosevelt*.

Roosevelt Lake is a lake in the center of Idaho with a town under it. All the Thunder Mountain books had been around that lake in one form or another, so I figured it was time to call one of the books by the lake name. Thus the title.

So I sat down, typed in the title, and grabbed a character name out of a phone book from some faraway city and typed in that as the first two words of the story.

And since I live on the Oregon Coast I figured why not just set the opening here? That thought flashed across my mind from somewhere unknown.

So I started typing. I had the character enjoying the fantastic beauty of the Oregon Coast and going into a small café in a small Oregon Coast town.

Café had great smells, of course. Great tastes, the ocean air, the sounds of the waves, and the warmth of the late summer day. I had all five senses and I layered them in really thick, giving my character's opinions of the setting with hints of what she was doing there.

Character.

Setting.

Then I ended the chapter and did the same thing with a male character in chapter two who was following the first character.

Character.

Setting.

And it went from there.

I stuck two characters in two chapters in rich, thick setting that they had opinions about.

Did I know where the book was heading? Nope, other than I figured at some point they would make it back to Idaho.

Did I know the characters? Nope, just learning about them as I typed.

Just as a reader would learn about them as the reader reads the book.

HOW TO GET STARTED WRITING INTO THE DARK

Take any character and put the character in a setting.

Any character.

Any setting.

Then climb into the character's head and park your butt there and don't allow yourself to type one word that doesn't come from the character's opinion or sensory feelings or emotions.

Stay parked inside that character's head.

And let the character (and the reader) experience the story.

CHAPTER SIX

SOME PROCESS HINTS

In this chapter, I'm going to talk about some process hints before we go any farther.

Remember, trust the process.

That takes a belief system in your own work. Of course, believing in our own work is where the critical voice hits us all the hardest. And where our wall against the critical voice is the weakest.

But writing into the dark takes a belief system in story. It takes a trust that your creative voice knows what it is doing. And it takes a vast amount of mental fight to walk against all the myths and let the fine work your creative voice has done alone and not ruin it with rewriting.

Writing into the dark also takes a complete awareness that uncertainty is part of the process, a normal part, not something to be feared.

Remember, if you start focusing on the uncertainty too much, you allow the critical voice to come in and stop you cold.

So you have to know uncertainty is part of the process, but not focus on it or care about it.

So now to some hints about major areas we all run into while writing into the dark.

PLOT TIME JUMPS

First off, when dealing with time jumps in a plot you don't know, remember that it is fine to write extra words. You should have no fear of writing extra words. Writing extra words is often part of the process.

So in the book I talked about in the last chapter, I ended up having three major time jumps in it.

Of course, when writing the book I didn't know that. But as I was writing, working my two characters in alternating chapters through their journey, it became clear from what I had set up that there needed to be a section break and a time jump. The characters basically had nothing to do that was interesting for an entire year.

But where to jump to? When to jump to?

Without some sort of idea where the story was even heading, I had no idea.

So I kind of sat there and looked at what I had written and went, "It seems logical they would jump to this point in time."

So I jumped there, put them back into a rich, thick setting with depth, and started typing. About two thousand words in I discovered the point where I should have jumped the characters.

I shrugged, cut off the extra words I had written, and just kept on going.

I was not afraid to write extra and just explore.

Back to the exploring a cave analogy. When exploring into the dark, we are often faced with two possible paths: one cave goes to the right, one to the left. We have no idea what is ahead, so we pick one and explore.

If it's the wrong path, we back up and go the other way.

Part of the process.

Have a belief in the process, and jumping ahead in a story will never be a problem.

BOGGING DOWN

Every writer I know bogs down in a story at one point or another. For me, and for most writers, it means we have done one of two things.

First, we have written past an ending of a chapter or scene, and the creative voice is just going to make us stop typing.

Second, we are on a wrong path with the plot. (Wrong branch of the cave.)

The subconscious, when it realizes you have taken a bad path, will just bog you down and stop you from typing.

What I do when this happens is simple. I look back at what I have written in the last three or four pages.

Writing past an ending on a scene or chapter is usually very, very clear. The ending almost always just pops off the page.

So I cut off the extra typing, do the scene or chapter break, and head forward with the characters.

When I am on a wrong path, I go back searching for the branch in the cave, keeping that analogy going.

When I find the one spot where I could have gone another direction, I cut off the extra words and go off in the new direction. I'll know I'm going in the right direction because suddenly the story is flowing again faster than I can type.

So bogging down is part of the process as well.

Expect it and don't be afraid to write extra words or cut words to get back on track.

END OF BOOK

When you bog down near the end of a book or a story, it often means you have written past your ending.

I do that all the time on short stories. I'll be typing along with the sense that the ending should be coming up soon and then I'll just bog down. Usually I'll sit there trying to figure out the end before I have the realization to look back a little bit at what I have already typed.

Often, more times than not, the great ending is back a hundred words or so. I wrote it and then just kept typing.

THE ONE-THIRD POINT OF A NOVEL

On novels, almost every writer I know hits a stopping point about one third of the way into writing the book. It does not matter if you are writing into the dark or outlining—this one-third point is a deadly spot for all novelists.

And most beginning writers working at their first novel never make it past this spot. This one-third point stopped me on all my first attempts. On every novel, I still have troubles with it.

The reason I want to mention it in a book on writing into the dark is because this one-third point stop is often blamed on writing into the dark. Blamed on not having an outline.

It has nothing to do with it.

Nothing.

Here is basically what happens:

As writers, we are all excited as we get started into a novel. The characters are fun and new, the promise of the novel is like a shining star, the words are all golden, the story flowing like a perfect stream, everything is just powering along.

Then you hit that one-third spot.

Suddenly, your critical voice comes roaring in. And it's loud. Damn loud.

Everything you have written, all those golden words, suddenly look like crap. The middle boring part of the book is ahead, or if you are writing into the dark, the fear of not knowing what is next rears up and becomes a monster.

And then the critical voice hits you with the thought, "This book is so bad, so much work to finish, what's the point?"

That's the end of the book. It goes into the unfinished file with a promise to yourself you'll come back to it, but of course you never do.

Critical voice has killed the book dead.

Critical voice: 1. Writer: 0.

There have been some amazing articles written by professional writers about this spot in a novel. It really is a deadly spot.

So how do you get through it?

There is only one way.

Suck it up and write the next sentence.

And then the next.

You must be aware that this stopping point in a book is part of the process and you can't let the critical voice in the door to kill it.

There are no easy solutions.

And sucking it up is not an easy solution.

Just keep writing, shove the critical voice down into the corner again, believe there will be value in your work, and stay inside the character's heads and keep writing.

Do not let yourself make any stupid promises to yourself. You are still writing the book, period.

Don't get sloppy because the writing suddenly got difficult.

Just stay with the characters and stay in their heads and write the next sentence.

Trust your process.

Eventually, the excitement will return and you'll find the end and be very glad you kept going.

CHAPTER SEVEN

UNSTUCK IN TIME

There is one critical element in learning how to be a creative writer and writing into the dark with larger projects. And this one element sounds simple, but is extremely difficult to take in and learn for almost all early writers. That's right. You are going to think you know this, but you won't apply it.

You must learn how to be unstuck in time in your book.

Let me see if I can explain this critical element to learning how to write into the dark. And in all creative fiction writing, for that matter.

And then in the next chapter, I'll use this very idea to show you how to drive your writing forward.

READERS READ FROM FRONT TO BACK

That's an obvious point, isn't it? We readers all pick up a book, start on page one, and read to the end of the book and put the book down because the story is over.

There is a straight line through the book. Front to back.

Reading is a very lineal process.

And we are all readers.

So when we come to writing, we have the experience as readers. After all, we've read thousands and thousands of books, haven't we? We believe that from front to back must also be the experience of the writing process.

We believe, without ever questioning, that we must write the book just as the readers will read it.

So as beginning writers—and I was no exception to this rule early on—we try to write novels from the first word to the last word.

We believe, and are taught by people who don't know any better, that the writing process is a lineal process from word one to the last word.

This false thinking is what leads to the driving need for outlining.

This false thinking is what leads to the driving need for rewriting by beginning writers. Their critical voice cannot let them believe it is possible to write a book from word one to the end without mistakes.

Why is that belief there?

Because, as readers, when we picked up a book we loved, we read from word one, and we all thought the author was so smart as to put all that nifty stuff in, and clues, and foreshadowing, and no character got lost, and wow it all came together in this nifty climax at the end.

Wow, that writer was really smart.

So as early writers, we think, "I'm not that smart. I don't know story that well, or plot, or any of that other stuff English teachers teach, so I have to rewrite to put all that in."

Then, of course, to rewrite, we go back to the beginning and start through the book again like a reader.

Front to back.

The reading process is a lineal process.

The truth is that the creative process is far, far, far from lineal.

In fact, when looked at in a hard light, the creative process is a jumbled mess.

REMEMBER YOU ARE WRITING YOUR ONLY DRAFT OF THE BOOK

That is critical to remember and keep firmly in mind before I go any farther. More than likely you dismissed that in an early chapter, but right now is when this becomes a critical point.

You must fix everything as you go because there will be no second chance, no second draft, no rewrite.

So with that firmly in mind, you are typing along and you realize you forgot some important detail, or forgot to dress a character, or forgot to plant a gun.

If there will be no rewrite, what do you do?

You fix it right at the moment you think of it.

You go up out of the lineal line of your book, float over that lineal line like a creative ghost. And then go back in the lineal timeline of your book and fix the problem.

Then fix the problem all the way through to where you left off and go from there again.

All problems your creative voice thinks of **MUST BE FIXED AT ONCE.** You are writing in creative voice. Stay in creative voice and fix the issues the creative voice comes up with instantly.

If you write some dumb note to fix it later, or think it will be fixed in second draft, you undermine all the wonderful stuff your creative voice is doing.

Your creative voice, at that moment, thought of that need to fix a problem.

Fix it. Honor your creative voice.

If you don't you almost kill the creative voice right there and you let in the critical voice.

When the creative voice knows the critical voice will mess up something, it's like a little kid. It will just say "What's the point?"

And stop.

So get unstuck in the timeline of your book and be willing to jump around at will to do what the creative voice wants you to do.

WRITE AHEAD, WRITE IN PIECES, CONSTANTLY LOOP

There are so many ways that long-term professional writers do this unstuck-in-time creative process.

Some, such as my wife, often write a project in pieces. She's writing into the dark, no idea where she is going, and she listens to her creative voice.

If her creative voice wants her to write a scene, she writes it. And often she'll have parts of a book, all written out of order, and when her creative voice tells her, she prints them all out and puts it all together on the floor.

Some writers I know have a scene appear to them, they write it, then loop back and write toward the scene.

I constantly loop back every 500 words or so, and I'll talk more about that process, called *cycling*, next chapter.

Remember, the key is that you (as a writer) are unstuck in the timeline of your book.

That's right. Let me free you up right here.

There is no rule that says you must write your book like a reader is going to read it.

None.

Get unstuck in time.

BUT SOMETIMES STRAIGHT THROUGH IS THE BEST WAY

I tend to build most of my books from front to back. But if you diagramed out how my eye actually works, what I actually typed, as I write a book that feels like it is lineal, you will discover my writing is far, far from lineal.

I will write a few hundred words, loop back, fill in some other stuff, take out some other words, write forward from the place where I lifted out of the timeline, then loop around again and do it all again.

It feels to me at times like I am starting at the beginning and moving toward the end. But in all honesty, it's more like digging a tunnel through a mountain.

I dig for a little bit, go back, take out the dirt, shape the tunnel a little, dig a little farther, go back, take out the dirt, shape some more, dig some more, and so on.

Eventually I find the end of the tunnel and when I look back I have created a wonderful, smooth-sided tunnel. And that's what the readers think when they walk through the tunnel from one end to the other.

But sure not what the process was.

The belief that we MUST write a book straight through is what grinds writers down.

And what makes many writers believe in all the people who say we must outline.

Logical, actually.

If you believe, deep down, that the only real way to write a book is from word one to the end, then outlining is more than likely something you are going to have to do.

And plan for a short career.

For all of us, the reader must experience our book in a lineal fashion. And we are all readers. So this drive to write from front to back is strong.

But even if you start with word one on a novel and write lineal forward, kill your fear of jumping out of the book and be like a floating god over the characters and the path of the book and let your subconscious have that freedom.

When you can write in any fashion you want, you are not roped into traveling from word one to the last word in the writing process.

And that gives your creative voice the freedom to build that lineal process for the reader in any way it wants.

WRITE THE NEXT SENTENCE

That's advice I gave to help you through the rough points, the stuck points.

A key point to remember is that "next sentence" does not have to be the very next sentence the READER is going to read. It just needs to be the next sentence you are going to type.

The next sentence could be the start of the next chapter.

Or you could cycle back and write some extra description at the start of chapter two as the next sentence.

It all makes your book longer, it all pushes the book forward.

Sometimes the next sentence when you are stuck will be the next sentence the reader will read.

But often it won't be.

And it sure doesn't have to be to help you keep going.

UNSTUCK IN THE TIMELINE
OF YOUR STORY

Again, this is the most critical point about writing into the dark, or even becoming a full-time professional storyteller.

You must realize you are the writer of your book, not the reader of your book.

You are unstuck in time in your own book.

In other words, you can jump around in your manuscript at will.

Creative minds do not tend to work in a straight line.

And as a writer, you don't need to.

All that matters is that the reader experiences your story in a straight line from word one to the end.

But no one cares if you write it that way.

And chances are, you won't.

Or shouldn't.

CHAPTER EIGHT

THE HINT OF CYCLING

Very little that is created is created lineally.

But in writing, our audience experiences a very clear order to a book. And if that order isn't clear, they leave the book.

So it is logical that new writers come at writing thinking they must create the book just as a reader experiences the work.

But thankfully, it doesn't work that way, as I talked about in the last chapter.

Or, at least, it doesn't have to.

MODERN COMPUTER AGE

The modern computer age has been both a blessing and a curse for writers. In the days of typewriters, or writing by hand, rewriting was a chore, to say the least, so professional writers quickly learned to not do much rewriting. Especially the top storytellers who were working for a certain amount per word.

They didn't get paid for rewriting. Only finished product.

The focus was to get it correct the first time through.

That should still be your focus, even though rewriting is easy in this new computer world, and myths of modern publishing expect it.

But back before the computers of the last 25-plus years, making a mistake and fixing it on a typed page was a pain. I know I personally went through bottles of Wite-Out because of my spelling and bad typing.

And the rule of thumb when submitting a manuscript to an editor was no more than ten corrections on a page. If you had more than ten, you had to retype it. And trust me, ten fixed mistakes on a manuscript page looked awful, so I retyped at five mistakes.

And I was a horrid typist. I hated typing, especially retyping. So my two-finger hunt-and-peck method was slow. Very slow.

But now the fixes are easy.

And that causes the problem of too much rewriting.

But it also allows professional writers a wonderful tool that many, many of us have adopted. The tool is called cycling.

Now to understand this tool and use it correctly, you have to be completely unstuck in the timeline of your manuscript. Timeline of the manuscript is page one, followed by page two, and so on until the end of the book.

Those page numbers should mean nothing to you until the end of the book, and even the order of the chapters should mean little to you.

In creative mode, nothing is set in stone.

You are not locked into the moment you are typing. You can go anywhere in the story and type at any point in the manuscript.

CYCLING

I thought for the longest time that I was the only one who had picked this up. That's my ego for you. The more I talked with other professional writers, the more I realized that in one form or another, all of us did this.

Let me explain what I do, so you get a clear picture of what I am calling *cycling* and find a form of it that will work for you.

I start into what I think is the opening of a story or novel. I climb inside a character's head and get the emotions of the character about the setting around the character, and I type for two or three pages.

500 to 700 words or so.

And I come to a halt.

Every time, without fail. This is now a dug-in habit.

I instantly jump out of the timeline of the story and cycle back to the first word and start through the story again.

Sometimes I add in stuff, sometimes I take out, sometimes I just reread, scanning forward, fixing any mistakes I see.

(Remember, this will be the only draft I will do.)

So when I get back to the white space, I have some speed up and I power onward, usually another 500 or so words until I stop.

Then I cycle back again to the beginning and do the same thing, run through it all until I get back to the white space with momentum and power forward again for another 500 or 700 words.

Then I cycle back about 700 to 1,000 words and do it again.

So if you were tracking how I write a story or novel, you would see me go 500 words forward, back, power to the white spot again, more forward, then back.

I am completely unstuck from the timeline of the novel.

Sometimes, when I get a nifty thought, I type it and then write forward until I get there.

But almost always I cycle back, all in creative voice, never once judging the work, just working to make it clearer, make the character better, the setting richer, and so on and so on.

I could never do this with a typewriter.

Only the last 25 years or so since I got my first computer have I been able to do this.

HOW CYCLING HELPS
WRITING INTO THE DARK

When you have no idea where you are going with a story, momentum is often the key to it all.

I have great momentum for about 500 words, about two manuscript pages. Then I run into that "What happens next?" question.

So by cycling back, I am putting the character and the events solidly in my mind by going over them again. And when I hit the white space where I stopped, I have momentum to drive the story forward.

By going back and coming forward again, my creative voice knows what's going to happen next.

When I am really, really stuck, I often will cycle back a full chapter or so and take a run at the stuck spot, spending 15 minutes or so going over what I have done, touching it, getting my creative voice back into where it was going.

More often than not, that solves being very stuck.

Think of this as the white spaces being small hills and I need to get a run at each hill. And think of being very stuck as a larger hill, and I need to back up farther to get more speed at the larger hill.

FIXING MISTAKES

Cycling, knowing you will be done when you hit the end, makes you fix any problem or mistake instantly, the moment you see or discover the problem.

So say a character says something to another character and your creative voice goes, "Damn it, that wasn't set up."

You instantly pop out of the timeline and go back and set it up and then work toward the white space again.

You need to have a character wearing something different for a plot reason that came up in chapter four, you instantly go back and fix what the character is wearing, moving forward again through the manuscript until you get to the white space to make sure all the details match.

You need to look up a detail, you stop, look it up, put it in, cycle back and run at the white space again to make sure the detail is correct.

DOESN'T CYCLING TAKES MORE TIME?

Seriously, I get this question a lot and I imagine some of you reading this are thinking it.

But no, this takes far, far less time to get a story right the first time through then to try to fix it later. And that goes for putting silly brackets around something you have to research later.

Get it right and be done and move on to a new story.

By having that attitude, you power up your creative voice to get it right the first time.

You don't write sloppy.

You don't write for a second draft.

Now are some of my first runs through 500 words sloppy? I don't honestly know. I suppose so because I am not paying any attention, and I know I will cover those 500 words to clean them up at least twice more, if not more than twice, in very short order.

But to be honest, I don't notice or care. My subconscious knows this will be the only time through and I'm known for moderately clean manuscripts. Not perfect. No manuscript is perfect.

But I'm fairly clean.

So how much time does this take me?

I tend to think I write (that's finished, after cycling) about 1,000 or so words per hour, typing with three fingers and taking five and ten minute breaks every hour or so.

Sometimes I am faster. Not slower that often.

If I had to worry about going back for a second draft, I doubt I would be writing. I know the story, so it would be boring because I know the story.

I didn't rewrite when I wrote on a typewriter either.

I never reread my stories after I get to the end.

Why?

Because I have seen every word in the story two or three or four times in the cycling.

And I know I don't have to.

CHAPTER NINE

HELPFUL HINT #2

The first major hint on writing into the dark was being un-stuck in time in your manuscript, learning to cycle.

So now, this second hint is to save you more time than you can imagine. It will help you be more productive and keep stress down.

And help you write better books.

Sounds magical, doesn't it?

Well, it sort of is.

OUTLINE AS YOU GO

I do not mean outline ahead in critical voice. Not in the slightest. Remember, you are writing in the dark.

I mean that when you finish a chapter, write down quickly what you just wrote in a very clear form.

Let me explain what I do so you can find a way that works for you.

When I finish a chapter, I have a yellow legal pad sitting beside the computer.

(I would suggest you use something like a legal pad instead of doing this on a screen. Save the screen for creative writing.)

On that yellow legal pad I mark the chapter number, the viewpoint character, what happened in the chapter (one-line summary) and how the chapter ended.

That usually takes one or maybe two lines on the legal pad per chapter.

On that page, or another piece of paper, I also have what the character is wearing, and if they change clothes, I make a note on the chapter line that they changed clothes.

So by chapter six, I have six or so lines on a notepad beside my computer telling me exactly where I have gone and what I have written so far.

This takes me about one minute to do, if not less, at the end of every chapter.

But, wow, does it save me hours of time.

MULTIPLE VIEWPOINT NOVELS

Most of the books I write are multiple viewpoint novels. And I write one character per chapter. I tend to make each scene a chapter. So if you are writing scenes inside chapters, do a line on your reverse outline for each scene.

If I am writing a thriller, which is often five to eight viewpoints, this outline as I go becomes even more important for me to remember the last time I was in a viewpoint.

Instead of looking back through the book to see what the character was wearing and where did I leave them in their last scene, I just glance at my notebook and go, "Oh, yeah."

In essence, that yellow piece of paper is an external memory drive for me.

The more complex the book or the plot as it develops, the more detail I put into this outline as I go.

I had one very complex book where each chapter was actually three lines on the yellow legal pad. So my outline took three pages or so of paper when it was all done.

WHY TAKE THE TIME?

Because not a one of us can hold an entire novel in our minds. We just can't. Not how the human brain works.

And because of that, many people say that's another reason to let the critical voice outline ahead.

But instead of doing that, just outline as you go.

Write into the dark and outline what you have done.

That way, at a glance you can see the novel on a single piece of paper beside your computer.

You can see what characters were wearing. And where they ended up in their last scene.

One reason for this is to save you hunting back through the novel after being away from it for some life event.

Say you are gone for a week and come back and sit down with no memory or the book or even where you are at. Hunting back through a couple hundred pages of manuscript to figure out what a character was wearing or what they were doing takes a vast amount of time and is very annoying.

And does not help in a restart after a life event.

With an outline as you go, you never have to look back in the manuscript, or if you do, you know which chapters to look in.

This saves vast amounts of time.

And keeps you far, far more productive and moving into the dark because you can see the novel building.

Seeing the novel building right there on the paper is great feedback to the creative voice.

SENSE OF NOVEL STRUCTURE

Again, we can't hold a novel in our minds, so later in the book you are writing, when you start worrying about the novel structure, whether are things moving too fast or too slow—you know, standard worry questions—you can glance at the outline page and just see the structure.

It is amazing how clear a structure becomes when just spread out in notes beside the computer, in a quick summary of what you have written.

(Another reason to not let this summary get too complex. Keep it simple and easy to see.)

And if there is a problem in the structure of the book, you can see that quickly as well.

I was doing this once with a big thriller: I got to chapter thirty and noticed on my outline I had a viewpoint chapter from a character in chapter four that I had never returned to.

Uh-oh. I jumped back, reread that character's chapter, realized I didn't need it, and cut it. My creative voice had put it in back at the start, but then decided I didn't need it by the middle of the book. I never would have noticed without that outline of what I had written.

Some of you have watched me write books here on this blog and then say the book got shorter because I cut out stuff.

So, since I never reread what I write after I get to the end, how do I know to cut out something?

Simple. It shouts at me from the structure of the outline that I wrote as I was writing.

I can see that everything is on track up until, say, chapter nine, then the characters go off and do something in a loop and return to the regular through-line of the book in chapter thirteen.

And the end of chapter nine fits perfectly against the start of chapter thirteen. Nothing really important happened in those loop chapters, so I just cut them out.

Not much work at all because I can see the structure clearly from the notes I made after I wrote each chapter.

So again, the quick outline of what I have written saves me a vast amount of time and makes the novels stronger.

So a helpful hint to make writing into the dark so much easier: Outline in a very concise, simple, and fast method, on a piece of paper beside your computer, what you have just finished.

Chapter or scene.

Just write it down and then get back to writing.

About halfway through the book, when you need to find something to fix or to figure out a character, you will thank me.

ONE FINAL NOTE

The moment I see the ending of the book—which for me is usually about four or five chapters away—I stop doing this outline as I go.

I no longer need it, and I never think to do it in the typing rush to reach the end of the novel.

And I never save the outlines unless the book is part of a series. Then I toss the outline and character details I have sketched down in a file for the next book in the series.

That hasn't helped much yet, but I keep doing it anyway.

The outline is for only when you are writing into the dark. After you are done with the story, most of the time that outline is worthless. It did its job.

It saved you time and energy, and helped you write a better book.

CHAPTER TEN

HELPFUL HINT #3

One of the things I hear the most from writers working into the dark is trouble finding the ending of the book or story. Or maybe better said, seeing the end of the book or story.

The ending is there. Recognizing it sometimes takes a special trick.

So let me try to ease some of the worry with this helpful hint.

JUST KEEP WRITING

I know that sounds silly, but it actually is the hint.

When you start feeling like your ending should be coming at any moment, but you can't see it, just keep writing until you bog down.

Then, when you bog down, cycle back about a thousand words and chances are you'll spot your ending about a page or two back. Then just cut off the stuff you wrote extra after the perfect ending line.

If you don't spot it, write another three or four pages and do it again.

Now, if you know your ending, of course don't do this.

But if you are having trouble finding that perfect ending line, just write and then cycle back and you'll see it.

I know, sounds magical, but it tends to work most times. It's part of the process of writing into the dark and trusting your subconscious.

Also, back to what I talked about in the beginning of the book: For this to work, you need to have no fear of writing extra.

Writing extra is part of the process and it applies right at the ending. Just cut off the not-needed words and don't worry about it.

WRITING TO LENGTH

This is a modern world with a thousand ways to publish any book of any length, yet I often hear writers saying they want their next novel to be 60,000 words or some such silliness.

I shake my head and walk away.

When writing into the dark, just let the story be what the story wants to be.

Trying to write to some made-up word length is all critical voice, and that simple idea of wanting a book to be a certain length will pile in the critical voice and shut down the creative voice.

Let the story be what the story wants to be at the length it wants to be.

Trust your creative voice.

Write what you are passionate about or what you enjoy.

And to the length the story needs to be.

THE LAST KEY

To really be successful at writing into the dark, or with any creative fiction writing, you are always better entertaining yourself.

So let me give you a few hints to finish this book up. A few checkpoints to remember.

—Entertain Yourself

You are a reader, so write into the dark to entertain yourself. You are writing the story for yourself.

—Enjoy the Uncertainty

As a reader, you pick up the book and don't know the story or the ending. You are reading the book for the journey. There is uncertainty in that journey. When writing into the dark, there is uncertainty in the journey as well. Enjoy it. Welcome it.

—Write the Book You Want to Read

If you love a certain type of book or wonder why you haven't seen a certain type of book you used to love, write it. Back to the first point. Entertain yourself.

—Never Write for Anyone But Yourself

Basically, stop writing to market. If you entertain yourself, enjoy the uncertainty, and write the books you want to read, writing into the dark is a joy.

THANKS FOR READING

I sure hope this book helped some, and on your next book you'll write into the dark. You might be surprised at just how much fun it is.

And how much more productive you are.

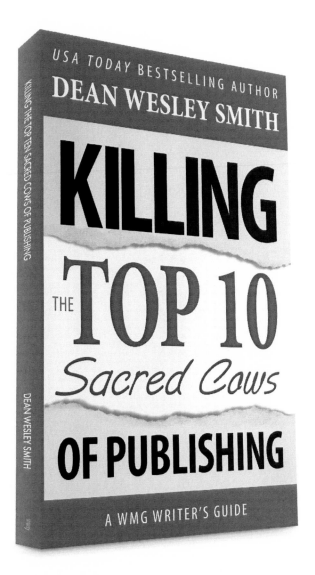

If you enjoyed *Writing into the Dark,* you might also enjoy *Killing the Top Ten Sacred Cows of Publishing,* available now from your favorite bookseller.

Turn the page for a sample.

Sacred Cow #1

THERE IS ONLY ONE RIGHT WAY TO DO ANYTHING IN PUBLISHING

That is the only way to do it."

How often do writers in this business hear that phrase? Some writer or editor or agent telling the young writer to do something as if that something was set in stone. Nope.

The truth is that nothing in this business is set in stone. *Nothing.*

And everything is changing so fast, what might have been true three years ago is very bad advice now.

For example, three years or so ago a wonderful new professional writer in one of the workshops here e-mailed a well-written query with ten sample pages and a synopsis of the novel off to an editor in New York from the workshop. The next morning she came out of her room smiling. Overnight, the editor had asked to see the entire book. So being am imp, I went to that publisher's website and printed off the guidelines, which said in huge letters *"No electronic submissions and absolutely no un-agented submissions."*

Lucky for her she hadn't bothered to look at the guidelines, or listen to all the people who said she needed an agent, or believed there was only one way to get her book read at that company.

Now, I would have asked her why she bothered even going to a traditional publisher.

Nothing in this business is set in stone. Nothing.

Of course, that little story about not looking at guidelines will cause massive anger to come at me I'm sure.

As will my question as to why she even bothered with a traditional publisher.

So before you go tossing bricks at my house because you need a rule to follow, let me back up and try to explain what I am saying here. And what I will be saying throughout this book. Then you can toss the brick.

All Writers Are Different

Perfectly good advice for one writer will be flat wrong for the writer standing beside him.

Some writers feel for some reason that they need an agent. Some writers need the control of indie publishing, but for some other writer that control would scare them to death. Some writers know business, other writers need help figuring out how to balance a checkbook and wouldn't understand cash flow in a flood of money.

So how do writers learn? And how can those of us who have walked this publishing road help out the newer professionals coming in? **Carefully** is my answer. But now let me try to expand on that.

How do writers learn?

1) Take every statement by any **WRITER**, including me, with your bull detector turned on. If it doesn't sound right for some reason, ignore it. It may be right for the writer speaking and wrong for you. And for heaven's sake, be extra, extra careful when you listen to any writer who is not a long distance down the publishing road ahead of you. Some of the stupidest advice I have ever heard has come from writers with three or four short story sales talking on some convention panel like they understand the publishing business and think that everything they say is a rule.

In fact, I get that all the time in e-mail. Honestly. Some beginning writer with a couple novels published is insistent that I am doing something wrong. I might be and I always keep an open mind and look at what they are saying. But most of the time it's the writer telling me in no uncertain terms I need an agent or need to publish in traditional publishing as they did. (I guess they forgot to look at my bio with over a hundred traditionally published novels behind me.)

So, when some advice doesn't feel right, check in with yourself and ask yourself where the concern is coming from. Is the concern that some advice isn't right in conflict with something you learned in school from someone who wasn't a writer? Or does the advice just not feel right for you. Check in with yourself on each thing you hear.

2) Take any statement by any **EDITOR** and run it through a very fine filter. Ask yourself why they are saying what they are saying, what corporate purpose does it fill, and can you use it to help you?

Remember, editors are not writers.

And they only know what they need in their one publishing house. Editors have the best of intentions to help writers.

Honest, they do. But they often do not understand how writers make money, and most think that writers can't make a living, since all they see are the small advances to writers they are paying. Just nod nicely when they start into that kind of stuff and move on.

And remember, they always have a corporate agenda. It's the nature of their job and who they work for.

3) Take any statement from an **AGENT** with a giant salt-shaker full of salt, then bury it with more salt. Then just ignore it. Agents are not writers; agents can't help you rewrite, and they only know about six or seven editors and nothing at all about the new world of indie publishing.

In this modern world, agents work for publishers, not you. If any agent is flat telling you that you must do something, and it sounds completely wrong to you, my suggestion to you is RUN! Remember, agents have an agenda. It is not your agenda. It is their agenda.

The day of agents in publishing is dropping away, finally. They are working for publishers or becoming publishers. So be careful when listening to what they are saying. There are many alternatives to needing an agent in this new world.

So how do writers learn?

—By going to lots and lots of conferences and listening to hundreds of writers and editors and taking only the information that seems right to you. This takes years. Think of it like going to college for four years. And after that the learning never stops.

—Read lots and lots of books by writers and only take what seems right for you.

—Read and follow lots of different publishing blogs, from publishersmarketplace.com to thepassivevoice.com to writer blogs like Kristine Kathryn Rusch's blog and Joe Konrath's blog. And then only take what information seems right to you.

—Learn business, basic business, and apply that to writing as well. Writing is a business, a very big business. Keep learning business and contracts and copyright as you go along.

—And keep writing and practicing and getting your work out to readers to get reader feedback.

How Can Professional Writers Help Newer Writers?

1) Professional writers, keep firmly in mind that your way, the way you broke in might be wrong for just about everyone else in the room listening to you. Especially today, when the world of publishing is shifting so fast it's hard for anyone to keep up. A story about your first sale in 1992 as a way to do it just won't be relevant in any real way to a new writer in 2014. Be clear that you understand that.

And remember, slush piles are gone. Writers are going directly to readers these days more and more. And then editors find them and make them offers.

And remember, the contracts you saw in 1990 and 2000 don't exist these days. Advances are much, much smaller and terms much, much worse. Don't give contract advice unless you see the contract and understand what the young writers are seeing. You will be stunned at what publishers are offering young writers these days.

2) Keep abreast of what the newer writers are facing. I get angry at times because newer writers keep accusing me of having some advantage. I don't, really. I have years more of practice, sure, and I have more work in inventory, and I understand business better than most, and I have a better work ethic than most writers on the planet.

But even with all that, I still have to get my work to readers in some fashion just as everyone else.

There is no secret road to selling to readers (or editors) just because you have done it before. I wish like hell there was, but alas, if it exists, I haven't found the entrance ramp yet. So to help myself, I keep abreast of what newer writers are facing, I help teach them how to get through the starting gate and become better storytellers, so I also know how to do it with my work. Duh. I learn from newer writers as I teach them.

3) Stay informed as to the changes in publishing and don't be afraid of the new technology.

Bragging that you belong to the Church of Luddite or that you won't touch any Apple product or that you hate smartphones sure won't instill a lot of confidence in the newer writers who live with this modern publishing world and use the new technology. And wishing things would go back to the way they were just doesn't help either.

And for heaven's sake, understand sampling and indie publishing and cover design and blurb writing and apps and all the basic skills needed by writers these days.

Newer Writers Need Set Rules

Writers, especially newer writers are hungry for set rules.

This business is fluid and crazy most of the time, and the need for security screams out in most of us. So in the early years we writers search for "rules" to follow, shortcuts that will cut down the time involved, secret handshakes that will get us through doors. It is only after a lot of time that professional writers come to realize that the only rules are the ones we put on ourselves. In my early years I was no different.

Writers are people who sit alone in a room and make stuff up. The problem we have is that when we get insecure without rules, we make stuff up as well.

When we don't understand something, we make something up to explain it. Then when someone comes along with a "this is how you do it" stated like a rule, you jump to the rule like a drowning man reaching for a rope. And when someone else says "Let go of the rope to make it to safety," you get angry and won't let go of that first safety line.

In all these chapters, that's what I will be trying to tell you to do: **Let go of the rope and trust your own talents and knowledge.**

When I first wrote these chapters online over almost three years ago, my suggestions caused some very "interesting" letters from writers mad at me for challenging their lifeline rules.

The desire for safety and rules is one of the reasons that so many myths have grown up in this business.

Rule upon rule upon rule, all imposed from the outside. Most are just bad advice believed by the person giving the advice at the time.

The key is to let go of the rope, swim on your own, and find out what works for you.

If you believe you must rewrite, write a couple dozen stories and get them out to readers without rewrites to see what happens. If you are having no luck finding an agent, send it to editors instead. Or better yet, indie publish it.

If you think you can't write more than 500 words a day, push a few days to double or triple that and see what happens. Push and experiment and find out what is right for you.

Will it scare you? Yes. But I sure don't remember anyone telling me this profession was easy or not scary. Those two things are not myths just yet.

Okay, all that said, here are a few major areas where following rules blindly can be dangerous to writers. I will talk about these in coming chapters. But for the moment, I want to touch on them right here because they are major.

1) "You must rewrite."

This is just silly, since writing comes out of the creative side of our brains and rewriting comes from the critical learned side.

Creative side is always a better writer. But again, this is different for every writer no matter what level. Some writers never rewrite other than to fix a few typos, others do a dozen drafts, and both sell. Those professionals have figured out what is best for them. But if a younger writer listens to someone who says you MUST rewrite everything, it could kill that writer's voice. This rule is just flat destructive. Keep your guard up on this one. Experiment on both sides and then do what works for you, what sells for you.

2) "You must have an agent."

This is such bad advice for such a large share of writers these days, it's scary.

These days there are many ways of not using or needing an agent.

—Using an intellectual copyright attorney is one way. Cheap and you don't have to pay them 15% of everything.

—Doing it yourself is fine as well.

—Indie publish it and let editors come to you.

3) "Editors don't like (blank) so you shouldn't write that way."

I can't begin to tell you how many thousand times I have answered questions like "Can I write in first person? Editor's don't like that." No rules, just write your own story with passion and then figure out a path to get it to readers.

If the readers don't like it, they simply won't buy it. No big deal. Stop worrying about what editors or agents want and write what you want. And then let readers decide.

Be an artist. Protect your work and don't let anyone in the middle of it.

Think for yourself, be yourself, write your own stuff. No rules.

4) "It's a tight market so you need to do (blank)." or "I need to figure out a way to get my fiction noticed in the noise."

You want a secret? It's always been a tight market and there has always been noise.

Right now there are more books being published every year than ever before, more markets, more ways for writers to make money. This silly "tight market" statement always sounds so full of authority coming from some young agent or editor. And it will drive a new writer into doing a dozen rewrites on a novel for someone who really doesn't know what they are talking about and couldn't write a novel themselves if forced to at gunpoint.

Again, my suggestion is stop letting others into your work and get it to readers. Let readers find it.

Truth: Publishing and readers are always looking for good books and new writers. And it has always been tight in one way or another. And there has always been noise.

Focus on what you can control such as how much you write, the quality of your own work, and where and how you get it to the most readers.

A Brand New World

Right now publishing is going through some major changes, all rotating around distribution for the most part. Writers have been so shut out with the system in New York that they are turning more and more to taking control of various aspects of their own work with indie publishing. POD and electronic publishing is allowing authors to become both writer and publisher and electronic distribution is allowing readers to find more work from their favorite writers, often either new work, dangerous work, or work long out of print..

This new area of publishing is quickly becoming full of "rules" and future myths. For the longest time publishing your own work was looked down on by "the ruling class" (whoever they are). Now, except for a few holdouts in the basements of the

Church of Luddite, writers are taking the new technologies and running with them.

Common sense: It takes a lot of practice to become a professional-level storyteller. You may think your first story or novel is brilliant because you rewrote it ten times and your workshop loved it, but alas, it might not be. In this new market, just as in the old one, the readers will judge. Let them, either through traditional channels or indie publishing. And then write the next book and the next and keep working to become better. Keep writing and learning.

It's called "practice" which is a term most writers hate.

Now I'm Taking the Rope Away

As I said above, writers tend to have this fantastic need for rules. We all want to make some sort of order out of this huge business. And actually, there is order if you know where to look and how to look. So instead of giving you rules, let me help you find order without myths and rules.

1) Publishing is a business. A large business run by large corporations in traditional publishing or your own home business when you are indie publishing. But it is always a business. If you remember that, learn basic business, understand corporation politics and thinking, learn copyrights, most everything that happens anywhere, from bookstores to distributors to traditional publishers, will make some sort of sense. Don't take anything personally. It's just business and that is the truth.

2) All writers write differently. And that includes you. My way of producing words won't be correct for anyone but me. So instead of listening to others looking for the secret, just go home, sit down at your writing computer, and experiment with every different form and method until you find the way that produces selling fiction that readers like and buy. Find your own way to produce words that sell.

3) Learning and continuing to learn is critical. This business keeps changing and the only way to stay abreast of the changes is to go out and keep learning and talk with other writers and find advice that makes sense to you and your way. Go to workshops, conferences, conventions and anything else you can find to get bits of learning. Read everything you can find about the business and the craft of telling great stories.

My goal has always been to learn one thing new every week (at least). I've been doing that since my early days and it has worked for me, and kept me focused on learning. Find what works for you.

I know those three things don't seem to give you any secrets, don't really show you the path to selling and getting readers to really want your work. But actually, they do. And if you just keep them in mind and don't allow yourself to get caught in strange rules and myths, you will move faster toward your goal, whatever that goal in writing may be.

It's your writing. It's your art. Stop looking for the secrets and stand up for your work.

Trust your own voice, your own methods of working. Get your work to editors who will buy it. Or indie publish it and let readers buy it. Or both.

And if your methods are not producing selling work that readers love, try something new.

Keep learning. Keep practicing your art.

The only right way in this business is your way.

Sacred Cow #2

WRITING FAST IS BAD

Or said in myth fashion: **WRITING SLOW EQUALS WRITING WELL.** Or the flip side: **WRITING FAST EQUALS WRITING POORLY.**

This comes out of everyone's mouth at one point or another in a form of apology for our work. "Oh, I just cranked that off."

Or the flip side… "This is some of my best work. I've been writing it for over a year."

Now this silly idea that the writing process has anything at all to do with quality of the work has been around in publishing for just over 100 years now, pushed mostly by the literature side and the college professors.

It has no basis in any real fact when it comes to writers. **None.** If you don't believe me, start researching how fast some of the classics of literature were written.

But don't ask major professional writers out in public. Remember we know this myth and lie about how really hard we do work. (Yup, that's right, someone who makes stuff up for a living will lie to you. Go figure.) So you have to get a long-term professional writer in a private setting. Then maybe with a few drinks under his belt the pro will tell you the truth about any project.

In my Writing in Public posts this year, I am doing my best to knock some of this myth down and just show what a normal day in a life can produce, even with me doing a bunch of other things at the same time.

My position:

NO WRITER IS THE SAME. NO PROJECT IS THE SAME.

And put simply:

THE QUALITY OF THE FINAL PRODUCT HAS NO RELATIONSHIP TO THE SPEED, METHOD, OR FEELING OF THE WRITER WHILE WRITING.

That's right, one day I could write some pages feeling sick, almost too tired to care, where every word is a pain, and the next day I write a few more pages feeling good and the words flowing freely and a week later I won't be able to tell which day was which from the writing.

How I feel when I write makes no difference to the quality of what I produce. None. Damn it, it should, but it just doesn't.

And I just laugh when a myth like this one attempts to lump all writers into the same boat and make us all write exactly the same way book after book after book.

No writer works the same, even from book to book or short story to short story.

In fact, as you will discover watching me over this year of writing in public, I don't do any story or novel similar to any other.

Talk to any writer, and I mean privately, and you will discover that one of the writer's books was written quickly, maybe even in a few weeks, while another book took the writer a half year to finish and he was deathly ill during half the writing time. And you, as a reader, reading the two books, would never be able to tell the difference.

But yet, traditional publishing, college professors, and just about anyone who even thinks about the writer behind the words has a belief system that words must be struggled over to be good.

Well, yes, sometimes.

And sometimes not.

Sometimes a writer gets into a white-hot heat and a book flows faster than the writer can type, getting done in just a number of days or weeks. And sometimes it just doesn't work that way.

Sometimes a writer has a deadline to hit and pushes to hit it, spending more hours in the chair, thus calling it writing fast. Some writers think and research a book for a few months, then write it in a few weeks. Some writers spend a month or two on a detailed outline, then take a month to actually write the book. Some writers start with a title, some write chapters out of order and then put it all together like a puzzle.

And on and on and on.

Every writer is different. Every writer's method is different *There is no correct, mandated way to write a book. Just your way.*

The Myth of Writing Slow to Write Better Actually Hurts Writers

There are two sides of our brains. The creative side and the critical side.

The creative side has been taking in stories since the writer started reading, knowing how to put words together at a deep level. The critical side lags far, far behind the creative side, learning rules that some English teacher or parent forced into the critical mind.

The creative side is always a much better writer than the critical side. Always. It never switches, no matter how long you write.

Long-term (20 years and up) professional writers have learned to trust that creative side and we tend to not mess much with what it creates for us. Of course, this lesson for most of us was learned the hard way, but that's another long chapter for another book.

A new writer who believes the myth that all good fiction must be written slowly and labor-intensive (called work) suddenly one day finds that they have written a thousand words in 35 minutes. The new writer automatically thinks, "Oh, my, that has to be crap. I had better rewrite it."

What has just happened is that the wonderful writing the creative side of the mind has just produced is then killed by the critical side, dumbed down, voice taken out, anything good and interesting removed.

All caused by this myth.

And professional editors in New York are no better, sadly. I once got a rewrite request on a major book from my editor. I agreed with about nine-tenths of the suggestions, so I spent the next day rewriting the book, fixing the problems, and was about to send the manuscript back when Kris stopped me.

The conversation went something like this:

"Don't send it, sit on it a few weeks," Kris said, looking firm and intense, as only Kris can look.

"Why not?" I asked, not remembering at that moment that the myth was a major part of traditional publishing.

"The editor will think you didn't work on it and that it is crap," Kris said.

"But I agreed and fixed everything," I said, starting to catch a clue, but not yet willing to admit defeat.

Kris just gave me that "stare" and I wilted, knowing she was completely correct.

I held the rewrite for three weeks, sent it back with a letter praising the rewrite comments and a slight side comment about how hard I had worked on them, even though I wrote most of another book in the period of time I was holding the rewrite. Story ended happily, editor was happy and commented on how fast I managed to get the rewrites done, all because Kris remembered the myth and how it functions.

Now, let me do something that just annoys people. I'm going to do the math.

The Math of Writing Fast

This chapter when finished is going to be around 2,000 words. That is about 8 manuscript pages with each page averaging 250 words per page.

So say I wrote only 250 words, one manuscript page per day on a new novel.

It takes me about 15 minutes, give-or-take (depending on the book and the day and how I'm feeling) to write 250 words of fiction. (Each writer is different. Time yourself.)

So if I spent that 15 minutes per day writing on a novel, every day for one year, I would finish a 90,000-plus word novel, a large paperback book, in 365 days.

I would be a one-book-per-year writer, pretty standard in science fiction and a few other genres.

15 minutes per day equals one novel per year.

Oh, my, if I worked really, really hard and managed to get 30 minutes of writing in per day, I could finish two novels in a year.

And at that speed I would be considered fast. Not that I typed or wrote fast, just that I spent more time writing.

God forbid I actually write four pages a day, spend an entire hour per day sitting in a chair! I would finish four novels a year. At that point I would be praised in the romance genre and called a hack in other genres.

See why I laugh to myself when some writer tells me they have been working really, really hard on a book and it took them a year to write? What did they do for 23 hours and 45 minutes every day?

The problem is they are lost in the myth. Deep into the myth that writing must be work, that it must be hard, that you must "suffer for your art" and write slowly.

Bull-puckey. Writing is fun, easy, and enjoyable. If you want hard work, go dig a ditch for a water pipe on a golf course in a steady rain on a cold day. That's work. Sitting at a computer and making stuff up just isn't work. It's a dream job.

Spend More Time in the Chair

Oh, oh, I just gave you the secret to being a "fast" writer or a "prolific" writer. Just spend more time writing.

I am the world's worst typist. I use four fingers, up from two, and if I can manage 250 words in fifteen minutes I'm pretty happy. I tend to average around 750-1,000 words per hour of work. Then I take a break. I am not a "fast" typist, but I am considered a "fast" writer because I spend more time writing than the myth allows.

That's the second thing that makes this myth so damaging to writers. It doesn't allow writers to just spend more time practicing their art. In fact, the myth tells writers that if they do spend more time working to get better, they are worse because they produce more fiction.

Writing is the only art where spending less time practicing is considered a good thing.

In music we admire musicians who practice ten or more hours a day. Painters and other forms of artists are the same. Only in writing does the myth of not practicing to get better come roaring in.

We teach new writers to slow down, to not work to get better, to spend fewer and fewer hours at writing, to not practice, and then wonder why so many writers don't make it to a professional level.

We No Longer Have to Wait for Traditional Publishers

For the last few decades, unless a writer wrote under many pen names, we were forced by the market to write fewer books per year. But now, with indie publishing, we can once again write as much as we want.

And we can write anything we want.

We can sell some books to traditional publishers, we can indie publish other books and stories. Or as I am doing, we can create our own market and indie publish almost everything.

The new world has lifted the market restrictions on speed of writing. Now those of us who actually want to sit and write for more than 15 minutes per day can publish what we write in one way or another.

And being fast, meaning spending more time writing, is a huge plus with indie publishing. We are in a new golden age of fiction, especially short fiction, and just as in the first golden age, writing fast (meaning spending more time at your art) will be a good thing also for your pocketbook.

Writing Slow Equals Writing Better is a complete myth, a nasty sacred cow of publishing that hurts and stops writers who believe it.

—The truth is that no two writers work the same and no book is the same as the previous book or the next book.

—The truth is that writing fast is nothing more than spending more time every day writing.

—The truth is that there should be no rule about speed relating to quality.

—The truth is there should be no rule that lumps all writers into one big class. There should only be your way of writing.

Be Careful!

Sadly, this myth is firm in the business, so writers who spend more time in the chair and who write more hours have to learn to work around the myth. We must learn to play the game that teachers, editors, book reviewers, and fans want us to play.

And if you decide you can spend more hours every day writing and working on your art, be prepared to face those who want you to write the way they do. Be prepared to face those who want to control your work. Be prepared to face criticism from failed writers (reviewers) who can't even manage a page a day, let alone more.

This speed myth is the worst myth of an entire book full of myths. Caution.

The best thing you can do is just keep your speed and your writing methods to yourself. Don't write in public as I am doing. You're an artist. Respect your way of doing things and just don't mention them to anyone.

Also, I beg of you that if you believe in the myth, please don't do the math about my age. I sold my first novel when I was 38 and have published over 100 novels. At one book per year, I must be at least 138 years old.

After my hard, single-page-of-writing every day, I sometimes feel that way.

Yeah, right.

But I stand by that story except when I am writing in public on my blog. (grin)

Sacred Cow #3

YOU MUST REWRITE
TO MAKE SOMETHING GOOD

That's one of the great myths of publishing. And one of the worst and most destructive to fiction writers.

First off, I want to repeat clearly what I said in the previous two chapters in different ways:

No writer is the same.

Let me repeat that with a few more words.

No writer works or thinks the same way, and there is no right way to work. Just your way.

That includes speed of writing, style of writing, and most importantly, how you handle rewrites of what you have written.

So, to make sure we are all speaking the same language, let me define a few terms that Kristine Kathryn Rusch and I have used for a long time now, and I will try to use in this discussion.

REDRAFT: That's when you take the typing you have done and toss it away, then write the story again from your memory of the idea. When you are redrafting, you are working from the creative side of your brain.

REWRITE: That's when you go into a manuscript after it is finished **in critical voice** and start changing things, usually major things like plot points, character actions, style of sentences, and so on. When you rewrite like this, you are working from the critical side of your mind. This often comes from fear or from workshop advice.

TOUCH-UP DRAFT: When you run through a manuscript fixing small things, things you wrote in notes while writing, things your trusted first reader found. Often very small things or typos. This draft takes almost no time, often less than half a day for a full novel, sometimes only an hour or so.

SPELL-CHECKING DRAFT: Since so many of us work with our grammar-checkers and spell-checkers off, we need a spell-check draft, often done before the manuscript is given to a first reader. This often takes an hour or so for a full novel.

Now, let me say right up front here that I am a three-draft writer. Most long-term pros that I have talked to in private are "three-draft" writers. Not all, since we all work differently, but a vast majority of the ones I have talked to use a process very near mine.

My process:

First draft I do as quickly as I can, staying solidly as much as possible in my creative side, adding in things I think about as I go along, until I get to the end of the draft. Again, I try to write as fast as the project will allow since I have discovered a long time ago that if I just keep typing, the less chance I have to get in my own way and screw things up.

Second draft I spellcheck and then give to my trusted first reader.

Third draft I touch up all the things my first reader has found and then I mail the novel or story.

If my first reader hates the story, I toss the draft away and redraft completely.

That's my process. I am a three-draft writer. (Unless I need to redraft, then I am a six-draft writer.)

More Basic Information About Writers

There is a way of describing and dividing writers into two major camps. Taker-outers and putter-inners.

In other words, a taker-outer is a writer who over-writes the first time through, then goes back and takes things out.

As a putter-inner, I write thin (my poetry background still not leaving me alone) and then as I go along, I cycle back and add in more and then cycle again and add in more, **staying in creative voice,** just floating around in the manuscript as I go along. Some people of this type make notes as they go along and then go back in a touch-up draft and put stuff in.

Okay, so terms done, on to the major topic.

So, what's the great myth about rewriting?

First, our colleges and our training and New York editors and agents all think that rewriting can make something better.

Most of the time that is just wrong.

Flat wrong when it comes to fiction. It might be right with poetry, or non-fiction or essays, but with fiction, it can hurt you if you believe this completely and let it govern your process.

Secondly, it makes writers think there is only one "right" way of writing.

And that if you don't fit into that way and rewrite everything, you are doing something wrong. That kind of thinking kills more good writers' careers than I can imagine, and I can imagine a great deal. And I have watched firsthand it kill more writer's dreams than I want to remember.

All writers are different, so sometimes a writer works with a ton of rewrites. Sometimes a writer just does one draft.

A Wonderful Conversation with a Master

One fine evening I was having a conversation with Algis Budrys about rewriting and why so many new writers believed the myth. He shrugged and said, "They don't know any better and no one has the courage to tell them." So I asked him if he ever thought rewriting could fix a flawed story. His answer was clear and I remember it word-for-word to this day: "*No matter how many times you stir up a steaming pile of crap, it's still just a steaming pile of crap.*"

If you ever worry about not "fixing" a story because you didn't rewrite it, just put that quote on your wall.

So, as an example, let's take some new writer hoping to write a book that will sell at some point. This new writer does the near-impossible for most new writers and actually finishes the book. That's a huge success, but instead of just sending the book off and starting on a second book, this poor new writer has bought into the myth that everything **MUST** be rewritten before it can be good. (It makes the new writer feel like a "real writer" if they rewrite because all "real writers" rewrite.)

All beginning fiction writers believe this myth, and you hear it in comments about their novel like "Oh, it's not very good yet. Oh, it needs to be polished. Oh, it was JUST a first draft and can't be any good."

I even hear that come out of some newer professional writer's mouths. I **never** hear it from long-term pros (over 20 plus years making a living).

Of course, for the beginning writer, the first book just isn't very good most of the time. Duh, it's a first novel. It might be great, but it also might be crap. (Let me refer you back to Algis Budrys' comment.) More than likely the first book is flawed beyond rescue, but the writer won't know that, and the first reader won't be able to help "fix" anything besides typos and grammar.

So, what is the new writer to do at this point with a finished novel?

Simple. Mail it to editors or indie publish it yourself.

That's right, I said, *"Mail it or publish it."*

Awkkk! Has Dean lost it?

I can just hear the voices in your heads screaming now...

"But, it's no good! It needs a rewrite! It might be a steaming pile of crap. I can't mail something that's flawed to an editor!"

Or you indie published writers are thinking...

"I can't publish a book that's flawed or readers will hate me!"

And thus the myth has a stranglehold on you.

The great thing about editors is that we can't remember bad stories. We just reject them and move on.

Most of us, over the years and decades, have bought so much, we have a hard time remembering everything and everyone we bought. So you have nothing to lose by mailing it and everything to gain, just in case it happens to be good enough to sell.

And if it isn't, **WE WON'T REMEMBER. Why? Because we didn't read it. Duh.**

And readers of indie published books have a wonderful thing called "sampling." And taste. If the book sucks, oh, trust me, no reader but your family will buy it. And at that point you don't have a "career" to kill anyway. (Future chapter on that myth.)

Just because the book is bad doesn't mean someone will come to your house and arrest you if you mail it or publish it. Editors do not talk about manuscripts that don't work and readers never buy or read them.

Honestly, no one can shoot you for publishing it.

So get past the fear and just mail it. Or publish it. You have nothing to lose and everything to gain. (What happens if it is wonderful and will make you a million?)

One true thing about writing that is a firm rule: **There is no perfect book.** (No matter what some reviewer wants to think.)

(Also, there is a very true saying about writers that I will deal with in another chapter. Writers are the worst judges of their own work. Why is that? Because, simply, we wrote it and we know what was supposed to be on the page. It might not be, but we think it is. We just can't tell. A future myth chapter.)

If You Don't Rewrite, How Can You Learn?

You have to write new material to learn. No one ever learned how to be a creative writer by rewriting. Only by writing.

So, after the story or book is in the mail or published, start writing the next story or book, go to workshops and writers' conferences to learn storytelling skills, learn business, and meet people.

Study how other writers do things.

But keep writing that second story or book.

And then repeat.

Trust me, the second one will be a lot better than the first one, especially if you just trust yourself and write it and don't fall into the myth of rewriting.

When the second one is done, go celebrate again, then fix the typos and such and mail it to an editor who might buy it or publish it yourself, and then start writing again.

A writer is a person who writes.

Rewriting Is Not Writing

Yeah, I know what your English Professor tried to tell you. But if your English Professor could make a living writing fiction, they would have been doing it.

Putting new and original words on a page is writing. Nothing more, and nothing less.

—Research is not writing.

—Rewriting is not writing.

—Talking to other writers is not writing.

And what you will discover that is amazing is that the more you write, the better your skills become. With each story, each novel, you are telling better and better stories.

It's called **"practice"** (but again, no writer likes to think about that evil word).

Well, if you want to be a professional fiction writer, it's time to bring the word "practice" into your speaking. On your next novel, make it a practice session for cliffhangers. Mail the novel and then work on practicing something different on the next story or novel. And so on.

Follow Heinlein's Business Rules

I believe that a writer is a person who writes. An author is a person who has written.

I want to always be a writer, so I have, since 1982, followed Robert Heinlein's business rules. And those rules have worked for many, many of us for decades and decades.

His rules go simply:

1) You must write.

2) You must finish what you write.

3) You must not rewrite unless to editorial demand.

4) You must mail your work to someone who can buy it.

5) You must keep the work in the mail until someone buys it.

Those rules do seem so simple, and yet are so hard to follow at times. They set out a simple practice schedule and a clear process of what to do with your practice sessions when finished. But for this chapter, note rule #3. Harlan Ellison added to rule #3. "You must not rewrite unless to editorial demand." *Harlan addition: And then only if you agree.*

And, of course, if you indie publish, substitute "publish" in #4 for "mail" and let reader's buy it. And then for #5 just keep it for sale.

Speaking of Harlan, many of you know that over the decades he has tried to prove this point (and many others) to people. He would go into a bookstore, have someone give him a title or idea, then on a *manual* typewriter, he would sit in the bookstore window and write a short story, taping the finished pages on the window for everyone to read.

He never rewrote any of those stories. He fixed a typo or two, but that's it. And many of those stories won major awards in both science fiction and mystery and many are now in college text books being studied by professors who tell their students they must rewrite. But Harlan wrote all first draft, written fast, sometimes in a window while people watched him type every word.

I know, I was going to publish a three-volume set of these award-winning stories written in public back when I was doing

Pulphouse Publishing. But alas, he was still writing them, a new one almost every other week at that point, and the book never got out before we shut down. He's done enough since then to fill two more books at least.

Every writer is different.

If you want more on Heinlein's Rules, I did an almost two hour lecture (15 videos) on how and why Heinlein's Rules work and how they worked for me over the decades. It's under the lecture series tab if interested.

So, How Come Rewriting Makes Stories Worse Instead of Better?

Back to understanding how the brain works.

The creative side, the deep part of our brain, has been taking in story, story structure, sentence structure, character voice, and everything else for a very long time, since each of us read our first book or had a book read to us. It's that place where our author voice comes from, where the really unique ideas come from.

The critical side of the brain is full of all the crap you learned in high school, everything your college teachers said, what your workshop said, and the myths you have bought into like a fish biting on a yummy worm. Your critical voice is also full of the fear that comes out in "I can't show this to friends." Or, "What would my mother think?" That is all critical side thinking that makes you take a great story and dumb it down.

In pure storytelling skill level, the critical side is far, far behind the creative side of your brain. And always will be.

So, on a scale of one-to-ten, with ten being the top, the creative skills of a new writer with very few stories under his belt, if left alone, will produce a story at about a six or seven. However, at that point the writer's critical skills are lagging far behind, so if written critically, a new writer would create a story about four on the scale. So take a well-written story that first draft was a seven on the scale, then let a new writer rewrite it and down the level comes to five or so.

I can't tell you how many times I have seen a great story ruined by a number of things associated with this myth.

For example, take a great story, run it through a workshop, then try to rewrite it to group think. Yow, does it become dull, just as anything done by committee is dull. (Workshop myth coming in a future chapter.)

I helped start and run a beginners workshop when I was first starting out. None of us had a clue, but we were all learning fast. I would write a story a week (all I could manage with three jobs at the time) and mail it, then turn it into my workshop for audience reaction.

That's right, I mailed it before I gave it to my workshop. Why? Because I had no intention of ever rewriting it. I followed Heinlein's Rules.

And I sold a few stories that the workshop said failed completely, which taught me a lot, actually. If I had listened to them, I never would have made some of those early sales.

If you would like to see a first draft of one of my early stories, pick up Volume #1 of *Writers of the Future*. I was in the middle of moving from Portland to the Oregon Coast , actually packing the truck, when my then-wife, Denie, asked me if I had the story done for *Writers of the Future* that Algis Budrys had told me was starting up. I said no, the mailing deadline was the next day and I didn't have time.

Thankfully, Denie insisted I go finish it while she packed. I didn't tell her that I hadn't even started it yet and had no idea what to write.

I put the typewriter (electric) on a partially dismantled desk on top of a large box, sat on the edge of the bed, and wrote the story from start to finish having no idea what I was writing or where the story was going. Three hours later I finished the story called "One Last Dance" and mailed it on a dinner break.

That's right, it was a first draft on a typewriter. No spell-checker, no first reader, nothing.

Algis Budrys and Jack Williamson loved it and put it into the first volume, and because of that story, I ended up meeting Kris a couple of years later after Denie and I had gone our own ways. I also got lots of wonderful trips and money and a great workshop from that three-hour draft. And now, twenty-nine years later the story is still in print and I'm still proud of it.

All because I had the courage to write and mail first draft. Because I followed Heinlein's Rules.

I trusted my creative skills, I trusted my voice, and I was lucky enough to have someone who gave me support at that point in the writing.

Another Example: Every year for years, editor Denise Little and I would prove that same point again to early career writers. We forced them to write a short story overnight to an anthology idea and deadline, and those quickly-written stories were always better than the ones the same writers wrote over weeks before the workshop. And many of those stories, first drafts, have been in published anthologies out of New York.

The problem was that even though Denise and I harped on that lesson for years, most of those writers would then just go home and right back to rewriting, making their stories worse. That's how powerful this myth is.

The creative side is just a better writer than the critical side, no matter what the critical side tries to tell you.

Remember, the critical side has a voice of restraint and worry. But the creative side, as Kris likes to say, is your two-year-old child. It has no voice of reason and no way to fight. But if you let the child just play and get out of its way and stop trying to put your mother's or father's or teacher's voice on everything it does, you will be amazed at what you create.

One More Point

Every writer is different, granted, but I have only met a few writers who really, really love to rewrite. Most find it horrid and a ton of work, but we all, with almost no exception, love to write original stuff.

If you can get past the myth of rewriting, writing becomes a lot more fun.

Following Heinlein's Rules is a ton of fun, actually. And you end up writing and selling a lot of stuff as well.

However, this myth is so deep, I imagine many of you are angry at me at this moment, and trust me, even if you get past this myth in private, out in public you will need to lie.

That's right, I just told a bunch of fiction writers to lie. Go figure.

Maybe you don't need to go as far as Hemingway and tell people that you must write standing up because writing comes from the groin or some such nonsense. (He loved screwing with new writers minds.) But you do need to hide your process.

I know one writer who at writers' conferences tells people with a straight face he does upwards of ten drafts. I knew better and one day, in private, I asked him why he said that.

He just shrugged. "I like making my audience happy, so I tell them what they want to believe about me. It makes them believe my books and stories are worth more if I tell them I rewrote them ten times."

In other words, even though the reality of professional fiction writing is often few drafts, readers still believe we must rewrite because they went to the same English classes we did. Duh.

So, out in public, you will hear me say simply that I am a three-draft writer. It's the truth. I write a first draft, I spell-check the manuscript as a second draft, and I fix the typos and small details my first reader finds as a third draft.

And after 100 plus novel sales and hundreds of short story sales, it seems to be working just fine.

For me, anyway.

Every Writer Is Different

If you are rewriting and not selling, try to stop rewriting for a year and just mail or publish your work. You might be stunned at what happens.

Just remember, the writing process has nothing to do with the finished work.

Never tell anyone you "cranked that off" or that it's a "first draft." Let them believe you worked like a ditch digger on the story, rewrote it 50 times, workshopped it a dozen times, and struggled over every word for seven years. Won't hurt your readers.

But getting rid of this myth for yourself sure might help your writing.

And make writing a ton more fun as well.

To read more, pick up a copy of *Killing the Top Ten Sacred Cows of Publishing* from your favorite retailer.

ABOUT THE AUTHOR

USA Today bestselling writer Dean Wesley Smith published more than a hundred novels in thirty years and hundreds of short stories across many genres.

He wrote a couple dozen *Star Trek* novels, the only two original *Men in Black* novels, Spider-Man and X-Men novels, plus novels set in gaming and television worlds. He wrote novels under dozens of pen names in the worlds of comic books and movies, including novelizations of a dozen films, from *The Final Fantasy* to *Steel* to *Rundown*.

He now writes his own original fiction under just the one name, Dean Wesley Smith. In addition to his upcoming novel releases, his monthly magazine called *Smith's Monthly* premiered October 1, 2013, filled entirely with his original novels and stories.

Dean also worked as an editor and publisher, first at Pulphouse Publishing, then for *VB Tech Journal,* then for Pocket Books. He now plays a role as an executive editor for the original anthology series *Fiction River.*

For more information go to www.deanwesleysmith.com, www.smithsmonthly.com or www.fictionriver.com.

Made in United States
North Haven, CT
26 November 2022

27328686R00071